The Countries

France

Bob Italia
ABDO Publishing Company

visit us at
www.abdopub.com

Published by ABDO Publishing Company, 4940 Viking Drive, Edina, Minnesota 55435.
Copyright © 2001 by Abdo Consulting Group, Inc. International copyrights reserved in
all countries. No part of this book may be reproduced in any form without written
permission from the publisher.

Printed in the United States.

Photo Credits: Corbis

Editors: Tamara L. Britton, Kate A. Furlong, and Christine Fournier
Art Direction & Maps: Neil Klinepier

Library of Congress Cataloging-in-Publication Data

Italia, Bob, 1955-
   France / Bob Italia.
     p. cm. -- (The countries)
   Includes index.
   ISBN 1-57765-494-3
    1. France--Juvenile Literature. [1. France.] I. Title. II. Series.

DC17 .I85 2001
944--dc21

                            2001022484

Contents

Allô!

Hello from France! France is Europe's third-largest country. France has a long, proud history and many famous leaders.

France's land has many different forms. Its climate varies widely among the different regions. This has created **habitats** for many kinds of plants and animals.

Most French people live in cities and towns. In the rural areas, people live on farms and in villages.

France is western Europe's most important agricultural nation. But manufacturing is the most important part of France's **economy**.

France is a **republic**. It is led by a president and a **prime minister**. Its national holiday is Bastille (bahs-TEEL) Day. French people like sports. They also enjoy art and **culture**.

Allô *from France!*

Fast Facts

OFFICIAL NAME: Republique Francaise
(French Republic)
CAPITAL: Paris

LAND
- Mountain Ranges: French Alps, Pyrenees, Jura Mountains
- Highest Peak: Mont Blanc 15,771 feet (4,807 m)
- Major Rivers: Siene, Loire, Rhine, Rhône

PEOPLE
- Population: 59,024,000 (2000 est.)
- Major cities: Paris, Marseilles, Lyon, Toulouse, Nice
- Official language: French
- Major religions: Roman Catholic, Muslim, Protestant, Jewish

GOVERNMENT
- Form of government: Parliamentary democracy
- Head of state: President
- Head of government: Prime minister
- Legislature: Parliament
- National anthem: "La Marseillaise"
- National flag: The Tricolor

ECONOMY
- Agriculture: Beef cattle, milk, wheat, grapes, sugar beets, potatoes, apples, hogs, chickens, eggs
- Manufacturing: Iron and steel, chemicals, automobiles, electronic goods, textiles and clothing, aerospace equipment, processed foods and beverages, railway equipment
- Mining: Iron ore
- Money: One franc equals one hundred centimes. In 2002, France will begin using the euro.

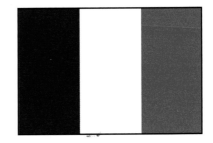

France's flag, the Tricolor

A franc and a French euro

Timeline

400s B.C.	Gauls settle in Paris
52 B.C.	Romans conquer France
late A.D. 400s	Franks conquer France
early 700s	Carolingian Dynasty rules France
late 800s	Vikings invade France
1066	William of Normandy conquers England
1453	French win Hundred Years' War
1789	French Revolution begins
1791	Revolution ends, France becomes a republic
1815	Napoleon I defeated at Waterloo; Congress of Vienna
1848	Second Republic begins
1875	Third Republic begins
1914-1918	World War I
1939-1945	World War II
1946	Fourth Republic begins
1958	Fifth Republic begins
1994	Channel Tunnel completed

History

The Gauls (gahlz) settled in Paris in the third century B.C. In 52 B.C., the Romans conquered France. Rome ruled France for more than 500 years.

In the late 400s, the Franks conquered France. They started the Merovingian (mehr-oh-VIN-gee-an) Dynasty. Clovis became the first Merovingian king. He made Paris the capital. In the early 700s, Franks formed the Carolingian (cahr-oh-LIN-gee-an) Dynasty. Charlemagne (SHAR-luh-mayne) was the most famous Carolingian king.

In the late 800s, Vikings invaded France. King Charles gave them the northeastern part of France, called Normandy. The Vikings became known as Normans.

In 1066, one of the Normans, William I, conquered England. But the Normans

Charlemagne

kept Normandy, too. The French tried to **expel** the Normans from France. This struggle is called the Hundred Years' War. The French won the war in 1453.

After their victory, France's kings worked to make France more powerful. King Louis XIV fought many wars and seized land all over the world. Later kings continued this expansion.

But the people disliked the high taxes that supported the wars. So on July 14, 1789, the people rebelled and started the French Revolution. The war ended in 1791, and France became a **republic**. This government is called the First Republic.

After the revolution, the army seized control of the government. Its leader, General Napoleon Bonaparte (nah-POH-lee-uhn BOHN-ah-pahrt),

King Louis XIV

became **emperor**. Under Napoleon I, France fought many wars and conquered many countries. In 1815, English, Austrian, and Prussian armies defeated Napoleon at the Battle of Waterloo.

In 1815, the Congress of Vienna took away much of the land France had conquered. The Revolution of 1830 restored the monarchy. Louis Philippe (loo-EE fee-LEEP) became king. In 1848, the people rebelled again. This began the Second Republic government.

Louis Napoleon Bonaparte became king in 1852. But he was not a good leader. In 1870, Germany defeated France in the Franco-Prussian War. In 1875, the people founded the Third Republic.

In 1914, **World War I** began. That year, Germany invaded France. There was heavy fighting. The war ended in 1918. France and its allies won the war. But more than 1 million French people died.

Germany started **World War II** in 1939. France and Great Britain declared war on Germany. In 1940, the Germans invaded France.

Part of the French army escaped to England. General Charles de Gaulle (day GAHL) organized this force. He worked with the United States and Russia to defeat the Germans. But the war left France in ruins.

Charles de Gaulle

General de Gaulle became president of a temporary government. In 1946, the Fourth Republic government was founded. But the presidency under this government was weak. So de Gaulle resigned.

During this time, France lost control of many of the countries it had conquered. In Asia and Africa, many

Georges Pompidou

colonies wanted independence. The French people argued over what to do. In 1958, de Gaulle became president again. This new government is called the Fifth Republic. De Gaulle worked out settlements in colonial territories.

Georges Pompidou (gehorge pohm-pa-DOO) was elected president in June 1969. He had been de Gaulle's **prime minister**. He promised to continue de Gaulle's policies. But he also worked more closely with the United States and the United Kingdom. Pompidou died in April 1974. Valery Giscard d'Estaing was elected president.

The voters elected **Socialist** Francois Mitterrand (frohn-SWAZE meet-TEHR-ahnd) as president in 1981. The new Socialist leaders greatly increased government ownership of businesses.

In 1988, Mitterrand won a second term as president. In May 1991, Mitterrand named Edith Cresson as France's first female **prime minister**.

In 1995, Jacques Chirac (JOK scher-AHK) became president. He worked to reduce France's high unemployment rate.

Today, France is a stable and prosperous nation. It has a strong **economy**. Its diverse population and strong **culture** make France an exceptional place to live and work.

Francois Mitterrand

France's Land

France is in western Europe. Its varied land has many climates. Most of France has hot summers and cold winters.

France's land contains the three major land forms found in Europe. They are lowland basins, highland plateaus, and mountain ranges.

The lowland basins are low-lying areas. They include France's river valleys. These areas have rich soil. France's largest basin is the Paris Basin.

France's highland plateaus are made of old mountain ranges that have **eroded**. The plateaus have steep hills and rocky soil. France's largest highland plateau is the Massif Central (mahs-EEF cehn-TRAHL).

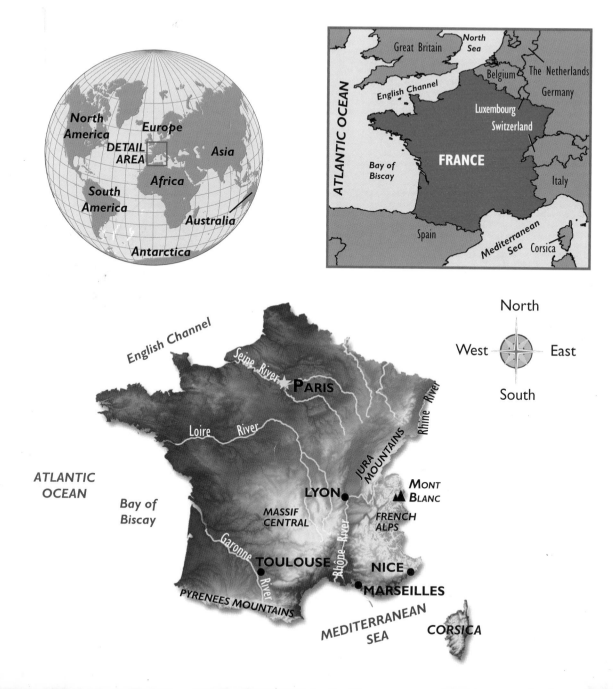

North

West — East

South

English Channel

Seine River

★ **PARIS**

Loire River

Rhine River

JURA MOUNTAINS

ATLANTIC OCEAN

Bay of Biscay

MONT BLANC

LYON ●

MASSIF CENTRAL

FRENCH ALPS

Garonne River

Rhône River

TOULOUSE ●

NICE ●

MARSEILLES ●

PYRENEES MOUNTAINS

MEDITERRANEAN SEA

CORSICA

Great Britain

North Sea

ATLANTIC OCEAN

English Channel

Belgium

The Netherlands

Germany

Luxembourg

Switzerland

FRANCE

Bay of Biscay

Italy

Spain

Mediterranean Sea

Corsica

North America

Europe

DETAIL AREA

Asia

Africa

South America

Australia

Antarctica

France has three major mountain ranges. The Pyrenees (PEER-uh-neez) extend along France's border with Spain. The French Alps and Jura Mountains border Italy and Switzerland. Mont Blanc (mohnt BLAHNK) is the highest point in France.

France's Rhine River is the main inland waterway in Europe. The Loire (la-wahr) River is about 650 miles (1,050 km) long. It is France's longest river.

Mont Blanc is 15,771 feet (4,807 m) high.

Rainfall

AVERAGE YEARLY RAINFALL

Inches		*Centimeters*
20 - 40		50 - 100
40 - 60		100 - 150
60 - 80		150 - 200

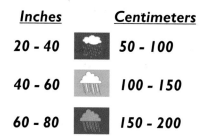

North
West   East
South

Temperature

Winter

AVERAGE TEMPERATURE

Fahrenheit		*Celsius*
68° - 86°		20° - 30°
50° - 68°		10° - 20°
32° - 50°		0° - 10°
Under 32°		Under 0°

Summer

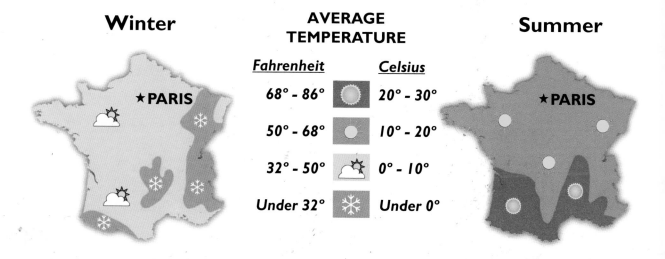

Plants & Animals

France's varied land has created **habitats** for many kinds of plants and animals.

Oak and beech trees are France's most common trees. Pine, spruce, and fir trees grow in higher elevations. Olive trees grow along the Mediterranean Sea. France's lower elevations have low-growing shrubs.

France's only major natural grassland is the Rhône River **delta**. It is called the Camargue (cah-MAHRG).

Many animals live in France. Deer are common throughout the country. Chamois (sham-ee), ibex, and brown bears live in the Alps and Pyrenees. Wild sheep live on Corsica. Wild pigs live in many parts of the country. Red foxes, wildcats, skunks, marmots, and mink also call France home. Beavers are rare and protected by law.

France's birdlife includes rollers, bee eaters, and blue rock thrushes. Ducks, geese, hawks, rooks, starlings, thrushes, and robins often spend the winter in France.

The Camargue is the only region in Europe where flamingos nest.

The French

Most people living in France are French. But France also has many people from other backgrounds. The largest groups are from Algeria, Southeast Asia, Italy, Morocco, Portugal, Spain, Tunisia, and Turkey. French is the country's official language.

Most French people are Catholic. There are also many Protestant groups in France. There is a small Jewish community. And immigrants from France's colonies have created a large Muslim population.

Most French people live in cities and towns. In the larger cities, most people live in apartments. There are many new houses outside the cities. In rural areas, people live on farms and in villages.

Opposite page:
A Muslim family
from Paris

Children ages two to six may attend free nursery schools. Then they go on to elementary school. After five years, they go to a college. A French college is similar to an American junior high school.

After college, students enter either a **vocational** high school or a general high school. These schools are called *lycees* (lee-SAYZ).

Lycees prepare students to take the *baccularreat* (bahk-you-lahr-ee-AHT). This difficult test demonstrates a student's knowledge. Students who pass may go on to a university or professional school.

French students at school

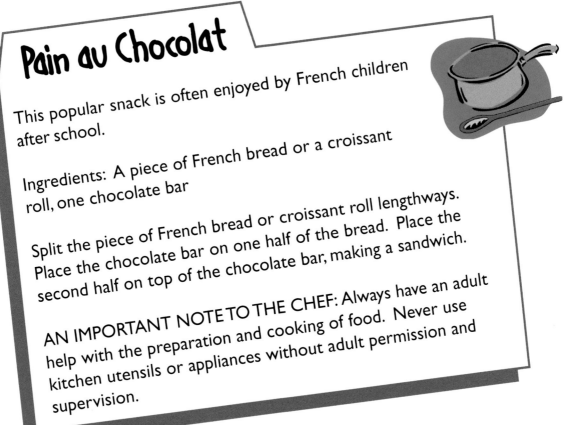

Pain au Chocolat

This popular snack is often enjoyed by French children after school.

Ingredients: A piece of French bread or a croissant roll, one chocolate bar

Split the piece of French bread or croissant roll lengthways. Place the chocolate bar on one half of the bread. Place the second half on top of the chocolate bar, making a sandwich.

AN IMPORTANT NOTE TO THE CHEF: Always have an adult help with the preparation and cooking of food. Never use kitchen utensils or appliances without adult permission and supervision.

English	French
Yes	Oui
No	Nulle
Thank You	Merci
Please	S'il vous plaît
Hello	Allô
Goodbye	Au revoir
Mother	Mère
Father	Père

LANGUAGE

Economy

France is the most important agricultural nation of western Europe. Wheat is the leading crop. French farmers also grow corn, barley, oats, and rye.

On the northern edge of the Paris Basin, farmers grow sugar beets and potatoes. Normandy and Brittany produce dairy products, early spring vegetables, and apples.

The nation's major wine producers are in the south. Peaches, plums, apricots, and tomatoes are also grown there.

Manufacturing is the most important part of the French **economy**. France is a world leader in automobile manufacturing and nuclear technology. Rapid transit, aircraft design, and tourism are also leading industries.

France depends heavily on imported fuels. But France is looking to alternative energy.

In the 1990s, there were more than 50 nuclear reactors in France. Only the United States generates more nuclear energy.

Cities

Paris is France's capital and largest city. The Siene (sen) River flows through Paris. Paris has many beautiful parks.

The Paris area is France's chief manufacturing center. It is also the country's **cultural** center. The palaces of France's kings are in Paris. It is home to many cathedrals, museums, libraries, and orchestras.

Marseilles (mahr-SIH) is France's second-largest city and its leading seaport. Marseilles's chief industries include petroleum refining, shipbuilding, and metalworking.

Lyon (LEE-ohn) is France's third-largest city. It is a center of financial and cultural activity. It stands where two great rivers, the Rhône (rohn) and the Saône (sahon), meet.

A passenger ferry on the Siene passes by the Notre Dame Cathedral in Paris.

Transportation

Paris is the country's main bus and train hub, with services to and from every part of Europe. A vast subway system called the Metrô carries Parisians all over the city.

In 1994, French and English workers completed the Channel Tunnel. The "Chunnel" has high-speed shuttle trains that transport people and cargo under the English Channel between England and France.

Rail traffic is also important in France. High-speed trains travel between Paris and Lyon in only two hours. High-speed train service is expanding to other lines as well.

Paris is the second-busiest European air travel center, after London. Air France, France's national carrier, and many other airlines link Paris with every part of the globe.

Passenger ferries and hovercraft travel over the sea to England between Calais (cahl-AY) and Dover, and Boulogne (boh-LOHN) and Folkestone.

Passengers at a Metrô Station

Government

France's federal government is a **republic**. It has three branches. They are the executive branch, the legislative branch, and the judicial branch.

The president is the head of the executive branch. The president serves a seven-year term. Beginning in 2002, the president will serve a five-year term. The president can serve an unlimited number of terms.

The president chooses a **prime minister**. The prime minister chooses the Council of Ministers and directs the daily operations of the government.

The legislative branch consists of a parliament made up of the National Assembly and the Senate.

The Constitutional Council makes up the judicial branch. Its nine members serve nine-year terms.

Locally, France is divided into **96** departments. Each department is governed by a general council and a **prefect**. The departments are divided into more than 30,000 communes. Each is governed by a mayor and a council.

The Parliament meets at the Palais-Bourbon in Paris.

Holidays & Festivals

In France, people celebrate both religious and **secular** holidays. Important religious holidays include the last day before **Lent**, when the French celebrate Carnival. The Carnival celebration in Nice includes a colorful parade.

On Easter, children receive colored candy eggs and chocolate chickens. On Christmas, French families hold reunions and the children receive gifts.

In addition to religious celebrations, the French people celebrate many secular holidays. On New Year's Day, French families and friends exchange gifts.

The French national holiday is celebrated on July 14. It is called Bastille Day. It marks the capture of the Bastille, a prison in Paris, during the French Revolution. There is a large military parade in Paris on Bastille Day. At night, people watch fireworks and dance.

The Cannes Film Festival in May, the International Music Festival in June, and the Jazz Festival in October draw visitors from all over the world.

Fireworks explode over the Eiffel Tower on Bastille Day.

Sports & Leisure

French people like sports. France has many world-class sports teams. The most popular sports are soccer, rugby, tennis, skiing, and cycling.

A famous cycling race is held in France. It is called the Tour de France. The Tour de France began in 1903. The race covers 2,500 miles (4,000 km) through many countries.

Skiing is also popular. Some of Europe's finest downhill ski resorts are in the French Alps. The Massif Central is good for cross-country skiing.

The Tour de France

The French people work to preserve French **culture**. They value literary and artistic creativity. There are many great French writers. Victor Hugo, Honoré de Balzac, (hohn-OR dey bhal-ZACK), and Marcel Proust (mahr-CEHL PROOST) are among France's best.

Henri Matisse

Painting is an important art form in France. French artists Edgar Degas (EHD-gehr day-GAH), Pierre Auguste Renoir (PEE-ehr ah-GOOST rehn-WAHR), and Claude Monet (CLAWD mohn-AY) were among the artists who started the Impressionist movement. Impressionist paintings attempt to show realistic light and color.

In the 1900s, such painters as Georges Braque (gehorge BHRAK), Henri Matisse (ahn-REE mah-TEESE), and Fernand Leger (fehr-NAHND lee-GAY) helped shape modern art.

Jean Antoine Houdon (jahn an-TWAN hoo-DAHN) was one of the greatest sculptors of the 1700s. He was known for his statues of important men and women in Europe and America. Auguste Rodin (ah-GOOST roh-DAHN) was a leading sculptor of the 1800s.

The Eiffel Tower was built for the World Fair of 1889. Named after its designer, Gustave Eiffel (goo-STAHV eye-FELL), it stands 1,050 feet (320 m) high. The Notre Dame (NOHT-rah DAHM) cathedral is one of the greatest achievements of Gothic architecture.

France has many museums to preserve its cultural heritage. The Musée du Louvre (mhu-SEE doo LOOVE) is a public museum. Its rooms are full of paintings, sculptures, and antiquities. The Centre Georges Pompidou displays modern and contemporary art. It is the most visited site in Paris.

The Musée de Louvre was constructed around 1200 as a fortress and rebuilt in the mid-sixteenth century for use as a royal palace. It became a public museum in 1793.

Glossary

culture - the customs, arts, and tools of a nation or people at a certain time.

delta - the area of land found at the mouth of a river. The land is made of silt, sand, and pebbles.

economy - the way a nation uses its money, goods, and natural resources.

emperor - the ruler of an empire.

expel - to drive away.

erode - to wash or wear away.

habitat - a place where a living thing is naturally found.

Lent - the 40 weekdays before Easter.

prefect - a chief government officer.

prime minister - the chief official in certain governments.

republic - a form of government in which power lies with the people and elected officials and not a king or queen.

secular - not related to the church.

Socialist - a person who favors a system where the means of production and distribution of goods is owned by the government.

vocational - a school that provides training in a skill, trade, or occupation.

World War I - 1914-1918. Fought in Europe. The United States, Great Britain, France, Russia, and their allies were on one side. Germany, Austria-Hungary, and their allies were on the other side. The war began when Archduke Ferdinand was assassinated.

World War II - 1939-1945. Fought in Europe, Asia, and Africa. The United States, Great Britain, France, the Soviet Union, and their allies were on one side. Germany, Italy, Japan, and their allies were on the other side. The war began when Germany invaded Poland.

Web Sites

French Embassy
http://www.info-france-usa.org/kids/
This informative site from France's embassy in Washington, D.C., has information on France's history, geography, culture, and language. Get fast facts about France and take a French language lesson here! Parlez-vous Français?

Meet Kids from France
http://teacher.scholastic.com/glokid/france
Learn about France and read questions and answers from French elementary school students at this site from Scholastic.

These sites are subject to change. Go to your favorite search engine and type in "France" for more sites.

Index

$21.35

DATE			